MW01713903

THAI
Food

R&R Publications Marketing Pty Ltd

CONTENTS

the land AND ITS PEOPLE

Status	Constitutional Monarchy
Area	514,000 sq km
Population	61,818,000
Language	Thai, English, regional dialects
Religion	Buddhist, Muslim, Christian
Currency	Baht
National Day	December 5

"The rice is pregnant!"

The jubilant cry echoes across fertile plains, through verdant valleys and over rugged mountains clad with teak trees and thick vegetation, terraced if a paddy can be possibly planted in the land of smiles. Smiles are wider when the top of the rice plant swells and the people see the first burgeoning shoots.

And as they grow, the jade green rice fields move like happily expectant women, heavily graceful in breeze in one direction, then another, as if a huge, heavenly hand has stroked them with tender encouragement to produce abundantly and well.

Geographically and culturally distinctive, Thailand's north was once known as Lanna, the land of a million rice fields. Its streams tumbled south to join the life source, the great Chao Phraya river from which water was harnessed into streams and canal irrigation systems, transforming the barren central plains north of Bangkok into fields of fertility, patches of plenty and one of the world's lushest rice and fruit growing areas.

But before the full May rains, the pregnant rice must be transplanted from flooding paddies or the crop will be never be born. Eveyone helps, almost knee deep in muddy water, bending, bending, picking, picking, enough to break the back of a robust man or woman, let alone a slight subsistence farmer and his wiry wife.

With its floral symbol the orchid, Thailand's most hard-working and most respected animal is the elephant, laudably, but only in recent years, being saved from extinction. Resembling the head and trunk of the gentle giant on a map, Thailand is bordered by Burma to the west, Laos and the Mekong river, also Cambodia, east, and Malaysia, south.

The curving trunk may not be Thailand's rice bowl but, washed by the Andaman Sea, west, the Gulf of Thailand and South China Sea, east, the southern tropical beaches are not only most visited by tourist resort sun-seekers but embrace traditional, unspoiled fishing villages which yield succulent seafood and fish and, near the last vestiges of rainforest, coconut and fruits.

Of 60 million Thais, who have naturally assimilated into their midst

Chinese, Mon, Khmer, Laotian, Malay, Persian and Indian people, about 80 per cent are involved in agriculture. To some degree over time, newcomers have influenced the cuisine of the former Siam, known as Thailand, land of the free, since 1932. This is despite many wars with neighboring countries, protracted skirmishes with Burma, World War II occupation by the Japanese and being the major R & R destination for American armed forces during the Vietnam War. Yet Thailand has never been colonised.

While certain big city districts switched on red lights, to remain ever illuminated as a result of the Vietnam war, and fast food chains have made their inevitable incursions, the Thais have retained their independence, friendliness, modesty, customs, religious devotion (most are Buddhists) and cuisine which is the fastest-growing in popularity in the west for restaurant-hoppers and home cooks - and also one of the healthiest, varied and satisfying. Vegetarians delight in it and, to inspire the weight conscious, one rarely sees a fat Thai.

Thai CUISINE

About the size of France, some 510,000 square kilometres, Thailand has as many changes to its cuisine in its four major regions as France does.

But while France, (which once sought to annex Thailand), Portugal, Holland, (Dutch via Indonesia), and, more dramatically, China and the former Malaya (Malaysia), have had some influences on Thai cuisine, it remains distinctively individualistic in the world.

Thais have borrowed from India but substituted ghee with coconut oil and replaced any dairy products with coconut and its milk. Dairy products are few in Thailand. More soy than cow milk feeds the children in small quantities. Don't finish a Thai meal at home with a cheese platter. It will be uncharacteristic. Cattle is cultivated for meat.

Gradually, overwhelming Indian spices were reduced and substituted with subtler fresh herbs such as lemon grass and galanga. Based on recipes passed down through generations, the cuisine, combined with spirituality and harmonious traditions, also is believed to be a recipe for longevity. As Buddhists do not believe big portions of meat from large animals should be served whole, they have minced and shredded them to combine with herbs and spices.

Chilli is one of Thailand's most important ingredients but it was introduced in the 17th century by Portugese missionaries who gained the taste for it when serving in South America. Not native originally are tomatoes, celery, sweet peppers, potatoes and carrots but they too have become a part of the cuisine.

Many westerners think of Thai food as unpalatably hot. Untrue. It is fact that it can be spicy and pungent yet a Thai meal can be respectively hot, salty, bitter, sour, subtle and sweet, and always aromatic and colorful. But as all dishes are served simultaneously, spicy bites can be tempered down by complementary tastes. In Thailand's restaurants and in Thai restaurants throughout the world, chefs aim for simplicity, balance of flavors and artistic presentation, so much so that vegetable and fruit carving has been regarded as an art form since ancient times. Intending visitors to Thailand can organise carving as part of a Thai cooking course in luxury hotels and resorts during a visit, take a course at home or else be inspired by the illustrations in this book.

Thai cooking is quick, therefore

fresh goodness is guaranteed. Herbs and spices have medicinal properties. The catch is preparation time, the chopping, slicing and spice-grinding which can take hours. But rewards are tantalising, harmonious enjoyment and satisfaction.

There is no requirement, as in western households, to serve soup, appetisers, main dishes and side dishes piping hot. Room (warm) temperature will do. But rice must be steamed at the last minute, unless in a rice cooker which maintains heat and texture for five hours, and served fluffy and steaming hot.

With the exception of chopsticks for noodles, eating is with a fork and spoon with serving spoons for shared dishes. Essentials are a large frying pan or a wok, or two, a mortar and pestle for spice-grinding and/or a food processor to speed preparation.
A saucepan with tight lid and steamer for vegetables and rice are necessary. The well-equipped kitchen should have the rest, including a strainer and a sharp knife for chopping. Even poor Thais make an electric rice cooker a priority investment.

Four regional STYLES

While Thai food is regarded by westerners as one cuisine, it is divided into four, representative of each major region. Teak and elephant country, the north, of craggy forest-clad mountains, lush valleys and running rivers maintained independence till the early 1900s.
Its cuisine has been influenced by Burma and Laos plus its natural bounties of cool climate vegetables and fruit such as strawberries, apples and grapes unable to be grown on hot plains.

Affluent southerners holiday there in hot months, their base the city of roses, Chiang Mai. They enjoy the basic sticky (or glutinous) rice, lesser in demand in the south, particularly when it is part of a traditional Khan Toke dinner presented to visitors at restaurants which may include a cultural show as well as a meal of marinated grilled chicken, northern curry, deep fried pork crackling and fiery nam prik sauce.

Four regional STYLES

Sitting cross-legged or at tables suspended over pits, somewhat Japanese style, diners roll sticky rice into balls, dip them into nam prik and collect the food pressed into the balls by hand.

Fermented fish, fermented bean sheet and land crab sauce are seasonings to flavor northern dishes of fresh water fish, chicken, pork and beef, usually sauteed till soft. Sweetness comes only from greens or meat. In Chiang Mai, try Thai/ Burmese Kow Soy noodles, crisp fried and dipped in coconut and curry soup or, if you dare, Chiang Mai sausage, pork cured for three days and eaten uncooked.

North of Chiang Mai are six main hill tribes people in remote mountain villages. Colorfully, traditionally dressed in richly embroidered costumes, they live frugally from mountainous land with little contribution to its cuisine, perhaps except to produce viper vodka with the snake inside the bottle and to sell fruit and nuts by the roads. But it is notable that King Bhumiphol and Queen Sirikit have taken huge initiatives to dissuade these people from opium growing in a region embracing the notorious Green Triangle.

They are encouraged to grow tea, lychees and other fruits, also to make unique handicrafts for visiting tourists. An aside. Should you visit a hill tribe settlement, do not take sweets for the children. From a town grocer, bring healthy rice biscuits and many small cartons of milk for infants and so-grateful nursing mothers.

Roasted, grilled, boiled and made spicy and pungent, the food of I-San or the north-east comes from an arid, barren region which many people have been forced to abandon to find work south. But locally produced meats and vegetables, not cooked with coconut milk, are distinctive, with use of flavors of fermented fish, roasted rice and ground chillies. As in the north, the staple is sticky rice.

It is hoped that the King's initiatives in developing irrigation systems and experienting with new varieties of plants and seeds, plus dairy processes at his home farm at Chiltrilada Palace in Bangkok, will assist farmers in poor areas like I-San. In the meantime, frogs and grasshoppers will sustain and chillies used with greater abandon than elsewhere in Thailand.

The central region includes Bangkok and, with irrigation from rivers and canals, the area produces many foods year-round. Shaped by the traditions of royal households down the centuries, the cuisine is rice-based with flavors including fish sauce, shrimp (prawn) paste, spices and soy bean sauce.

Salty and in variations derived of anchovies, prawns, squid and fish, fish sauce cannot be substituted as the main savory flavor in Thailand's cuisine.

The central region embraces the east coast, including Pattaya, brought to notoriety as an American R & R playground but now an internatioal resort for all. South of Pattaya, the town of Rayong is the nation's main fish sauce producer. Ocean washes towards tropical backdrops where grow exotic fruits including mangosteen, rambutan, star fruit, mango and like-it-or-hate-it durian. It smells like hell and tastes like heaven.

The south, to the border, is influenced by Moslems from Malaysia blending culture with Thai Buddhists and injecting Malay food traditions. Beach sands fade into sea which yields an enormous variety of fish and seafood. Coconut is widely used.

Unparalleled fruits of the sea are found at picturesque Hua Hin where a holiday house was built for the royal household by King Rama VI. The resort deteriorated. But, now, with the restoration of the house which can be visited, and introductions of splendid resorts such as The Dusit Polo Club and health spas, Hua Hin has undergone renaissance. Its unspoiled waterfront is one of the nation's best for exquisite eating. Restaurants in shallows on stilts overlook the port and in and outgoing fishing fleets which stay at sea for at least three days and nights.

Crabs, lobsters, prawns, squid, clams, innumerable fish scooped fresh from tanks supply locals, visitors and, from the boats, Bangkok directly.

styles

Of all the courses cooked in Thailand, appetisers can be regarded as the most eclectic.
Thai appetisers are quite filling. Ideal as party finger food, combinations of two or three with rice and a soup can make a main meal as evidenced by millions of Thais who eat daily where several hawkers congregate.
Most appetisers are delicately spiced. But when chilli is not added, chilli sauce will accompany the serve and possibly nam prik sauce to be used as a dip. For a simple nam prik, mix crushed fresh chillies with fish sauce, a dash of lime juice, crushed garlic and a smidgeon of raw or roasted shrimp (prawn) paste.
This goes well with fried or steamed appetisers, steamed rice, vegetables and an omelette. Try it with the omelette on page 20.
Why not prepare for a weekend Thai brunch with friends using some of the appetising recipes to follow?

CHICKEN SATAYS

Ingredients

1 stalk lemon grass
1 onion, chopped
1 clove garlic, chopped
2 tsp ground coriander (cilantro)
1 tsp turmeric
juice of 1/2 lemon
salt and black pepper
3 skinless boneless chicken breasts, cut into 1cm/1/2 in cubes
1/2 cucumber, pared into ribbons with a vegetable peeler, to serve

For the satay sauce

1 small onion, chopped
1 clove garlic, chopped
1 tbsp groundnut oil
1 tsp chilli powder
150mL/1/4 pint coconut milk
75g/3oz roasted salted peanuts, finely ground
1 tbsp soft dark brown sugar
1 tbsp fresh lemon juice

Method

1. Peel the outer layer from the lemon grass and chop the lower white bulbous part, discarding the fibrous top. Blend to a paste with the onion, garlic, coriander (cilantro), turmeric, lemon juice and 1 teaspoon of salt in a food processor. Alternatively, grind the lemon grass, onion and garlic with a pestle and mortar, then mix in the other ingredients.
2. Place the chicken in a non-metallic bowl and coat with the paste. Cover and marinate in the fridge for 2 hours, or overnight. If using wooden skewers, soak them in water for 10 minutes.
3. To make the satay sauce, blend the onion and garlic to a paste in a food processor or with a pestle and mortar. Heat the oil in a heavy-based saucepan and fry the paste for 5 minutes, stirring. Mix in the chilli powder, then the remaining sauce ingredients. Bring to the boil, stirring, then simmer for 10 minutes.
4. Preheat the grill to high. Thread the chicken onto 8 skewers. Grill for 10 minutes, turning once, until cooked. Serve with the cucumber and satay sauce.

Serves 4

THAI FISH CAKES WITH PEANUT DIPPING SAUCE

Ingredients

350g/12oz skinless cod fillets
1 tbsp Thai red curry paste
1 tbsp Thai fish sauce
2 tbsp cornflour
1 medium egg, beaten
1 shallot, finely chopped
50g/2oz fine green beans, cut into 5mm/¼in lengths
groundnut oil for shallow-frying

For the dipping sauce

2 tbsp sugar
juice of 1 lime
1 clove garlic, finely chopped
1cm/½in piece fresh root ginger, finely chopped
1 tbsp roasted salted peanuts, roughly crushed
1 small red chilli, deseeded and finely chopped
2 tbsp light soy sauce

Method

1. Finely mince the cod fillets in a food processor or pound using a pestle and mortar. Add the red curry paste, fish sauce, cornflour and egg. Blend again briefly or stir until mixed.
2. Transfer the fish mixture to a bowl and mix together with the shallot and beans. Lightly oil your hands (the mixture is quite sticky), then divide and shape into 8 patties.
3. To make the dipping sauce, mix together the sugar and lime juice, stirring until the sugar dissolves, then stir in the garlic, ginger, peanuts, chilli and soy sauce. Set aside.
4. Heat 1cm/½in of oil in a large frying pan over a medium to high heat, then fry half of the fish cakes for 3-4 minutes on each side, until golden. Drain on kitchen towels, then cook the remaining cakes. Serve with the dipping sauce.

Serves 4

THAI FISH STICKS WITH CUCUMBER SALAD

Ingredients

4 spring onions, chopped small
handful of fresh coriander (cilantro)
450g/1lb cod loin or other skinless white fish fillet, cubed
3 tbsp red curry paste
1 tsp salt
2 tsp lime juice
1 large egg white
12 stalks lemon grass

For the salad

1/2 cucumber, peeled and very thinly sliced
4 tbsp white wine vinegar
4 tbsp white sugar
1 large red or green chilli, deseeded and finely chopped
1 small shallot, thinly sliced

Method

1. To make the salad, combine the cucumber, vinegar, sugar, chilli and shallot with 4 tablespoons of cold water. Cover and leave in a cool place until needed.
2. To make the fish sticks, blend the spring onions and coriander in a food processor until finely chopped, or use a hand blender. Add the fish, curry paste, salt and lime juice and blend until the fish is finely chopped. Add the egg white and continue blending until the mixture is stiff.
3. Divide the fish mixture into 12 portions, then carefully press each around a lemon grass stick, forming a 'sausage' shape. Preheat the grill to high. Place the fish sticks on a lightly oiled baking sheet, then grill for 6 minutes, turning once, until cooked and lightly browned on all sides. Serve with the cucumber salad.

Serves 4

RICE CAKES WITH LIME CRAB

Ingredients

2 cups/440g/14oz jasmine rice, cooked
30g/1oz fresh coriander (cilantro) leaves, chopped
crushed black peppercorns
vegetable oil for deep-frying

Lime Crab Topping

185g/6oz canned crab meat, well-drained
2 fresh red chillies, seeded and chopped
2 small fresh green chillies, finely sliced
1/4 cup/60 mL/2 fl oz coconut cream
2 tablespoons thick natural yoghurt
3 teaspoons lime juice
3 teaspoons Thai fish sauce (nam pla)
3 teaspoons finely grated lime rind
1 tablespoon crushed black peppercorns

Method

1. Combine rice, coriander (cilantro) and black peppercorns to taste, then press into an oiled 18x28cm /7x11in shallow cake tin and refrigerate until set. Cut rice mixture into 3x4 cm/1 1/4x1 1/2in rectangles.
2. Heat vegetable oil in a large saucepan until a cube of bread dropped in browns in 50 seconds and cook rice cakes, a few at a time, for 3 minutes or until golden. Drain on absorbent kitchen paper.
3. To make topping, place crab meat, red and green chillies, coconut cream, yoghurt, lime juice and fish sauce in a food processor and process until smooth. Stir in lime rind and black peppercorns. Serve with warm rice cakes.

Makes 24

BEEF CURRY PUFFS

Ingredients
625g/1$^1/_4$ lb prepared puff pastry
vegetable oil for deep-frying
sweet chilli sauce (for dipping)

Spicy beef filling
2 teaspoons vegetable oil
4 red or golden shallots, chopped
1 tablespoon mild curry paste
2 teaspoons ground cumin
500g/1 lb beef mince
2 tablespoons chopped fresh coriander (cilantro) leaves

Method
1. To make filling, heat oil in a frying pan over a high heat, add shallots, curry paste and cumin and stir-fry for 2 minutes. Add beef and stir-fry for 5 minutes or until brown. Remove pan from heat and stir in coriander (cilantro). Set aside to cool.
2. Roll out pastry to 3mm/$^1/_8$in thick and cut into 10cm/4in squares. With one point of the pastry square facing you, place 2-3 tablespoons of filling in the centre and lightly brush edges with water, then fold over point to meet the one opposite. Press together and roll edges to form a crescent-shaped parcel. Repeat with remaining pastry and filling.
3. Heat vegetable oil in a large saucepan until a cube of bread dropped in browns in 50 seconds and cook puffs, a few at a time, for 2 minutes or until puffed and golden. Drain on absorbent kitchen paper and serve with chilli sauce for dipping.

Makes 24

PORK SPRING ROLLS

Ingredients
24 spring roll wrappers, each 12$^1/_2$cm/5in square vegetable oil for deep-frying
sweet chilli sauce (for dipping)

Pork and coriander filling
2 teaspoons peanut oil
3 red or golden shallots, chopped
2 teaspoons finely grated fresh ginger
1 fresh red chilli, seeded and chopped
500g/1 lb pork mince
2 tablespoons chopped fresh coriander (cilantro) leaves
2 tablespoons kechap manis

Method
1. To make filling, heat peanut oil in a frying pan over a high heat, add shallots, ginger and chilli and stir-fry for 2 minutes. Add pork and stir-fry for 4-5 minutes or until pork is brown. Stir in coriander (cilantro) and kechap manis and cook for 2 minutes longer. Remove pan from heat and set aside to cool.
2. To assemble, place 2 tablespoons of filling in the centre of each wrapper, fold one corner over filling, then tuck in sides, roll up and seal with a little water.
3. Heat vegetable oil in a wok or large saucepan until a cube of bread dropped in browns in 50 seconds and cook spring rolls, a few at a time, for 3-4 minutes or until crisp and golden. Drain on absorbent kitchen paper and serve with chilli sauce for dipping.

Makes 24

HERBED VEGETABLE ROLLS

Ingredients

12 large Oriental rice paper rounds
sweet chilli sauce (for dipping)

Herbed Vegetable filling

2 cucumbers, seeded and cut into 5cm/2in strips
2 carrots, cut into 5cm/2in strips
60g/2oz bean sprouts
60g/2oz rice vermicelli noodles, cooked and drained well
30g/1oz fresh mint leaves
30g/1oz fresh basil leaves
15g/½ oz fresh coriander (cilantro) leaves
4 tablespoons chopped roasted peanuts
12 garlic chives with flower (optional)

Method

1. Dip a rice paper round into cold water, then place on a clean teatowel, to absorb any excess moisture.
2. To assemble, place a little of the cucumber, carrot, sprouts, noodles, mint, basil, coriander and peanuts along the centre of each rice paper round leaving a 2cm/¾in border. Place a chive (if using) across the centre so that the end with the flower hangs over one edge.
3. To roll, fold up one edge of rice paper over filling to form base of roll, then roll up to enclose filling. Repeat with remaining rice paper rounds, filling and chives. Serve immediately with chilli sauce for dipping.

Note: Traditionally the garlic chive pops out the open end of the roll as a garnish. Oriental rice paper is made from a paste of ground rice and water which is stamped into rounds and dried. When moistened the brittle sheets become flexible. It is used to make delicacies such as these rolls. Sold in sealed packets rice paper can be purchased from Oriental food stores.

Makes 12

COCONUT PRAWNS (SHRIMP) AND SCALLOPS

Ingredients

1 kg/2 lb large uncooked prawns (shrimp), shelled and deveined, tails on
3 egg whites, lightly beaten
90g/3oz shredded coconut
vegetable oil for deep-frying
1 tablespoon peanut oil
4 fresh red chillies, seeded and sliced
2 small green chillies, seeded, sliced
2 cloves garlic, crushed
1 tablespoon shredded fresh ginger
3 kaffir lime leaves, finely shredded
375g/12oz scallops
125g/4oz snow pea (mangetout) leaves or sprouts
2 tablespoons palm or brown sugar
1/4 cup/60mL/2fl oz lime juice
2 tablespoons Thai fish sauce (nam pla)

Method

1. Dip prawns (shrimp) in egg whites, then roll in coconut to coat. Heat vegetable oil in a large saucepan until a cube of bread dropped in browns in 50 seconds and cook prawns (shrimp), a few at a time, for 2-3 minutes or until golden and crisp. Drain on absorbent kitchen paper and keep warm.
2. Heat peanut oil in a wok over a high heat, add red and green chillies, garlic, ginger and lime leaves and stir-fry for 2-3 minutes or until fragrant.
3. Add scallops to wok and stir-fry for 3 minutes or until opaque. Add cooked prawns (shrimp), snow pea (mangetout) leaves or sprouts, sugar, lime juice and fish sauce and stir-fry for 2 minutes, until heated.

Serves 6

THAI VEGETABLE SOUP

Ingredients

1 tablespoon chilli oil
4 red or golden shallots, chopped
3 stalks fresh lemon grass, cut into pieces, or 1 1/2 teaspoons dried lemon grass, soaked in hot water until soft
4 slices fresh or bottled galangal or fresh ginger
8 cups/2 litres/3 1/2pt vegetable stock
250g/8oz firm tofu, cubed
125g/4oz oyster mushrooms
125g/4oz snake (yard-long) or green beans, chopped
30g/1oz bean sprouts
1 cup/250mL/8floz coconut milk
2 tablespoons fresh basil leaves
3 tablespoons finely chopped peanuts

Method

1. Heat oil in a saucepan over a high heat, add shallots and lemon grass and cook, stirring, for 3 minutes. Stir in galangal or ginger and stock, then reduce heat and simmer for 5 minutes.
2. Add tofu, mushrooms, beans, bean sprouts and coconut milk and cook over a medium heat for 4 minutes or until beans are tender and soup is heated. To serve, ladle into bowls and scatter with basil and peanuts.

Serves 6

CHILLI KUMARA SOUP

Ingredients

6 cups/1 1/2 litres/2 1/2pt chicken stock
3 stalks fresh lemon grass, bruised, or 1 1/2 teaspoons dried lemon grass, soaked in hot water until soft
3 fresh red chillies, halved
10 slices fresh or bottled galangal or fresh ginger
5-6 fresh coriander (cilantro) plants, roots washed, leaves removed and reserved
1 large kumara (orange sweet potato), peeled and cut into 2cm/3/4in pieces
3/4 cup/185mL/6fl oz coconut cream
1 tablespoon Thai fish sauce (nam pla)

Method

1. Place stock, lemon grass, chillies, galangal or ginger and coriander (cilantro) roots in a saucepan and bring to the boil over a medium heat. Add kumara (sweet potato) and simmer, uncovered, for 15 minutes or until kumara (sweet potato) is soft.
2. Remove lemon grass, galangal or ginger and coriander (cilantro) roots and discard. Cool liquid slightly, then purée soup, in batches, in a food processor or blender. Return soup to a clean saucepan and stir in 1/2 cup/125 mL/4 fl oz of the coconut cream and the fish sauce. Cook, stirring, over a medium heat for 4 minutes or until heated. Stir in two-thirds of the reserved coriander leaves.
3. To serve, ladle soup into bowls, top with a little of the remaining coconut cream and scatter with remaining coriander (cilantro) leaves.

Serves 4

CHICKEN AND COCONUT SOUP

Ingredients

3 cups/750mL/1 1/4pt coconut milk
2 cups/500mL/16fl oz water
500g/1 lb chicken breast fillets, cut into 1cm/1/2in thick strips
4cm/1 1/2in piece fresh galangal or ginger, sliced, or 6 slices bottled galangal
2 stalks fresh lemon grass, cut into 4cm/1 1/2in pieces, or 1 teaspoon dried lemon grass, soaked in hot water until soft
1 fresh coriander (cilantro) root, bruised
4 kaffir lime leaves, shredded
3 fresh red chillies, seeded and chopped
2 tablespoons Thai fish sauce (nam pla)
2 tablespoons lemon juice
fresh coriander (cilantro) leaves

Method

1. Place coconut milk and water in a saucepan and bring to the boil over a medium heat, add chicken, galangal or ginger, lemon grass, coriander (cilantro) root and lime leaves and simmer for 6 minutes.
2. Stir in chillies, fish sauce and lemon juice. To serve, ladle into bowls and scatter with coriander (cilantro) leaves.
   Note: This popular Thai soup is known as Tom Kha Gai. When dining in the traditional Thai manner soups are not served as a separate course but are eaten with the other dishes and rice.

Serves 6

THAI PRAWN (SHRIMP) SOUP

Ingredients

2 stalks lemon grass
300g/11oz whole raw shell-on prawns (shrimp), defrosted if frozen
1 tbsp vegetable oil
1 litre/1$\frac{3}{4}$ pints chicken stock
1 clove garlic, crushed
2$\frac{1}{2}$cm/1in piece fresh root ginger, roughly chopped
grated rind of 1 lime and juice of 2 limes
1 green chilli, deseeded and chopped
salt and black pepper
1 tbsp Thai fish sauce
1 red chilli, deseeded and sliced, and 2 tbsp chopped fresh coriander (cilantro) to garnish
Serves 4

Method

1. Peel the outer layers from the lemon grass stalks and chop the lower white bulbous parts into 3 pieces, discarding the fibrous tops. Shell prawns (shrimp), leaving tails attached and reserving the shells for the stock. Cut a slit along the back of each prawn (shrimp) with a sharp knife and remove the thin black vein. Rinse the prawns (shrimp), then refrigerate until needed.
2. Heat the oil in a large saucepan. Fry the prawn (shrimp) shells for 2-3 minutes, until pink. Add the stock, garlic, ginger, lemon grass, lime rind, green chilli and salt to taste. Bring to boil, then reduce heat, cover and simmer for 20 minutes.
3. Strain the stock and return to the pan. Stir in the fish sauce and lime juice and bring to the boil. Add the prawns (shrimp), reduce the heat and simmer for 3 minutes or until the prawns (shrimp) turn pink and are cooked through. Season with pepper and serve garnished with red chilli and coriander (cilantro).

"To market, to market to buy a fat pig." For Thais not part of the Moslem minority, it's indeed home again, home again, jiggedy-jig in whatever vehicle can transport piglet to be fattened or pork to be prepared perfectly. Next to pork, beef is popular, then lamb, a fair rarity, and goat from mountainous regions. In the northern mountains, hill tribes make the most of snake. Mainly minced, shredded or thinly sliced in accordance with Buddhist traditions mentioned earlier, meat is cooked in one large piece only if it is to be thinly sliced before serving. Like poultry, it lends itself to curry, a part of every Thai main lunch or dinner.
Should vegetarians be among you, masses of vegetables can be substituted for meat and tofu (beancurd) added if the dish lacks body.

MINTED PORK AND MANGO SALAD

Ingredients

1 tablespoon vegetable oil
500g/1 lb lean pork mince
60g/2oz canned water chestnuts, chopped
2 stalks fresh lemon grass, finely chopped or 1 teaspoon dried lemon grass, soaked in hot water until soft
2 tablespoons lime juice
1 tablespoon fish sauce
60g/2oz bean sprouts
3 spring onions, chopped
4 tablespoons chopped fresh mint
2 tablespoons chopped coriander (cilantro)
freshly ground black pepper
250g/8oz assorted lettuce leaves
2 mangoes, peeled and sliced
60g/2oz hazelnuts, roasted and chopped

Method

1. Heat oil in a wok over a medium heat, add pork, water chestnuts and lemon grass and stir-fry for 5 minutes or until pork is brown. Remove from wok and set aside to cool.
2. Place pork mixture, lime juice and fish sauce in a bowl and mix to combine. Add bean sprouts, spring onions, mint, coriander (cilantro) and black pepper to taste and toss gently.
3. Line a serving platter with lettuce leaves, then top with mangoes and pork mixture. Scatter with hazelnuts.
   Note: This salad can be prepared to the end of step 2 several hours in advance. Cover and keep at room temperature. If preparing more than 2 hours in advance store in the refrigerator and remove 30 minutes before you are ready to assemble and serve it.

Serves 4

THAI BEEF SALAD

Ingredients

500g/1 lb rump or topside steak
185g/6oz mixed lettuce leaves
185g/6oz cherry tomatoes, halved
2 cucumbers, peeled and chopped
2 red onions, sliced
3 tablespoons fresh mint leaves

Lime and coriander (cilantro) dressing

1 stalk fresh lemon grass, chopped or 1 teaspoon finely grated lemon rind
3 tablespoons fresh coriander (cilantro) leaves
1 tablespoon brown sugar
2 tablespoons lime juice
3 tablespoons light soy sauce
2 tablespoons sweet chilli sauce
2 teaspoons Thai fish sauce (nam pla)

Method

1. Heat a frying or char-grill pan over a high heat until hot, add beef and cook for 1-2 minutes each side or until cooked to your liking. Set aside to cool.
2. Arrange lettuce, tomatoes, cucumbers, onions and mint attractively on a serving platter.
3. To make dressing, place lemon grass or rind, coriander (cilantro), sugar, lime juice and soy, chilli and fish sauces in a bowl, mix to combine.
4. Slice beef thinly and arrange on salad, then drizzle with dressing and serve.

Serves 4

COCONUT BEEF CURRY

Ingredients

1 tablespoon vegetable oil
1 tablespoon Thai Red Curry Paste (see page 78)
500g/1 lb rump steak, thinly sliced
1½ cups/375mL/12fl oz coconut milk
2 zucchini (courgettes), sliced
1 red capsicum (pepper), chopped
125g/4oz cherry tomatoes
4 spring onions, sliced diagonally
12 fresh basil leaves

Method

1. Heat oil in a wok over a medium heat, add curry paste and stir-fry for 3 minutes or until fragrant. Add beef to pan and stir-fry for 5 minutes longer or until beef is brown.
2. Stir coconut milk into pan and bring to the boil. Reduce heat and simmer, stirring occasionally, for 15 minutes. Add zucchini (courgettes), red capsicum (pepper), tomatoes and spring onions and cook for 10 minutes longer or until beef is tender. Stir in basil leaves and serve.

Note: Remember if you do not have time to make your own curry pastes use commercially prepared ones available from supermarkets and Oriental food stores.

Serves 4

THAI CHILLI BEEF

Ingredients

750g/1 1/2 lb rump steak, cut into strips
2 cloves garlic, crushed
1 tablespoon finely grated fresh ginger
1 tablespoon Thai Red Curry Paste (see page 78)
1 tablespoon sesame oil
1 tablespoon vegetable oil
1 onion, cut into wedges
1 green capsicum (pepper), chopped
1 red capsicum (pepper), chopped
440g/14oz canned baby sweet corn, drained
220g/7oz canned bamboo shoots, drained
1 tablespoon Thai fish sauce (nam pla)
1 tablespoon brown sugar
1/2 cup/125mL/4fl oz beef stock

Method

1. Place beef, garlic, ginger and curry paste in a bowl and mix to combine.
2. Heat sesame and vegetable oils together in a wok over a high heat, add beef mixture and stir-fry for 5 minutes or until beef is brown. Remove beef mixture from pan and set aside.
3. Add onion to pan and stir-fry over a medium heat for 3 minutes or until golden. Add green capsicum (pepper), red capsicum (pepper), sweet corn and bamboo shoots and stir-fry for 5 minutes longer or until vegetables are tender.
4. Return beef to pan, stir in fish sauce, sugar and stock and bring to simmering. Simmer, stirring occasionally, for 10 minutes or until beef is tender.

Note: When handling fresh chillies, do not put your hands near your eyes or allow them to touch your lips. To avoid discomfort and burning, you might like to wear gloves. Chillies are also available minced in jars from supermarkets.

Serves 6

PORK IN GARLIC PEPPER

Ingredients

2 teaspoons vegetable oil
4 cloves garlic, sliced
1 tablespoon crushed black peppercorns
500g/1 lb lean pork strips
1 bunch/500g/1 lb baby bok choy (Chinese greens), chopped
4 tablespoons fresh coriander (cilantro) leaves
2 tablespoons palm or brown sugar
2 tablespoons light soy sauce
2 tablespoons lime juice

Method

1. Heat oil in a wok or frying pan over a medium heat, add garlic and black peppercorns and stir-fry for 1 minute. Add pork and stir-fry for 3 minutes or until brown.
2. Add bok choy (Chinese greens), coriander (cilantro), sugar, soy sauce and lime juice and stir-fry for 3-4 minutes or until pork and bok choy are tender.
   Note: Bok choy is also known as Chinese chard, buck choy and pak choi. It varies in length from 10-30cm/4-12in. For this recipe the smaller variety is used. It has a mild, cabbage-like flavour. Ordinary cabbage could be used for this recipe.

Serves 4

PORK AND PUMPKIN STIR-FRY

Ingredients

2 tablespoons Thai Red Curry Paste (see page 78)
2 onions, cut into thin wedges, layers separated
2 teaspoons vegetable oil
500g/1 lb lean pork strips
500g/1 lb peeled butternut pumpkin (squash), cut into 2cm/$^3/_4$in cubes
4 kaffir lime leaves, shredded
1 tablespoon palm or brown sugar
2 cups/500mL/16fl oz coconut milk
1 tablespoon Thai fish sauce (nam pla)

Method

1. Place curry paste in wok and cook, stirring, over a high heat for 2 minutes or until fragrant. Add onions and cook for 2 minutes longer or until onions are soft. Remove from pan and set aside.
2. Heat oil in wok, add pork and stir-fry for 3 minutes or until brown. Remove pork from pan and set aside.
3. Add pumpkin, lime leaves, sugar, coconut milk and fish sauce to pan, bring to simmering and simmer for 2 minutes. Stir in curry paste mixture and simmer for 5 minutes longer. Return pork to pan and cook for 2 minutes or until heated.
   Note: Spoons and forks are used in Thailand for eating, not chopsticks. Like most Europeans, Thais would only use chopsticks when eating Chinese food.

Serves 4

stir-fry

BEEF AND BEAN STIR-FRY

Ingredients

2 teaspoons vegetable oil
2 cloves garlic, crushed
500g/1 lb topside or round steak, cut into thin strips
185g/6oz snake (yard-long) or green beans, cut into 10cm/4in lengths
2 kaffir lime leaves, shredded
2 teaspoons brown sugar
2 tablespoons light soy sauce
1 tablespoon Thai fish sauce (nam pla)
2 tablespoons coriander (cilantro) leaves

Method

1. Heat oil and garlic together in a wok over a medium heat, increase heat to high, add beef and stir-fry for 3 minutes or until beef changes colour.
2. Add beans, lime leaves, sugar and soy and fish sauces and stir-fry for 2 minutes or until beans change colour. Stir in coriander (cilantro) and serve immediately.

   Note: Kaffir limes are a popular Thai ingredient. Both the fruit and the leaves have a distinctive flavour and perfume and are used in cooking. The leaves are available dried, fresh frozen or fresh from Oriental food shops and some greengrocers. If kaffir lime leaves are unavailable a little finely grated lime rind can be used instead.

Serves 4

LAMB IN MINT

Ingredients

1 medium eggplant (aubergine)
1 tablespoon salt
2 tablespoons oil
500g/1lb lean lamb, thinly sliced
2 cloves garlic, chopped
1 red chilli, seeded and chopped
fish sauce
2 tablespoons brown sugar, well packed
1/3 cup 80mL/2 1/2fl oz water
20 fresh mint leaves

Method

1. Cut eggplant (aubergine) into bite-sized chunks, place in a colander and sprinkle with salt, mix well and leave to drain for 20 minutes. Rinse under cold water and drain well.
2. Heat oil in a wok or large frying pan. Add lamb and garlic and fry until well browned (you may need to do this in batches). Add eggplant (aubergine) and chilli and stirfry over a moderate heat for 5 minutes.
3. Stir in fish sauce, brown sugar, water and mint leaves and fry for a further 1 minute or until eggplant (aubergine) is softened. If sauce becomes too thick, add a little extra water.
   Serve with steamed long-grain rice.

Serves 4

BARBECUED PORK

Ingredients

4 cloves garlic, crushed
150mL/5 fl oz light soy sauce
55g/2oz dark muscovado sugar
15mL/1tbsp grated root ginger
15mL/1tbsp chopped fresh coriander (cilantro) stems and leaves
4 whole star anise or 5mL/1tsp ground anise
red food colouring (optional)
2 pork fillets
30mL/2tbsp vegetable oil
2 shallots, chopped
115g/4oz ground roasted peanuts
150mL/5 fl oz pork or chicken stock
5mL/1tsp cornflour, mixed with a little water
lime leaves and star anise, to garnish

Method

1. Mix together the garlic, soy sauce, sugar, ginger, coriander (cilantro), anise and a few drops of food colouring, to make a marinade.
2. Place the pork fillets in a shallow dish and add the marinade. Turn the pork over so that it is fully coated and leave to marinate for at least 1 hour, turning once.
3. Remove the meat from the marinade and place on a trivet in a roasting tin. Roast in an oven preheated to 375°F/190°C/Gas 5 for 20 minutes, or until the pork is cooked. Baste once or twice with some of the marinade during cooking. Test the pork with skewer - the juices should run clear.
4. Just before the end of the roasting time, heat the oil in a wok and fry the shallots until tender and beginning to brown. Stir in the ground peanuts, the remaining marinade and the stock. Cook until simmering, then stir in the cornflour mixture and cook a little longer until thickened.
5. To serve, slice the pork and pour the sauce over. Garnish with lime leaves and star anise.
   Serving Suggestion: Serve with Thai Fried Rice.
   Variation: The pork can be cooked on a barbecue.
   Note: Traditionally, this dish would be cooked on charcoal burners by the roadside, but it works just as well in the oven.

Serve 4

RED BEEF CURRY

Ingredients

1 cup/250mL/8fl oz coconut cream
3 tablespoons Thai Red Curry Paste (see page 78)
500g/1lb round or blade steak, cubed
155g/5oz pea eggplant (aubergines) or 1 eggplant (aubergine), diced
220g/7oz canned sliced bamboo shoots
6 kaffir lime leaves, crushed
1 tablespoon brown sugar
2 cups/500mL/16fl oz coconut milk
2 tablespoons Thai fish sauce (nam pla)
3 tablespoons fresh coriander (cilantro) leaves
2 fresh red chillies, chopped

Method

1. Place coconut cream in a saucepan and bring to the boil over a high heat, then boil until oil separates from coconut cream and it reduces and thickens slightly. Stir in curry paste and boil for 2 minutes or until fragrant.
2. Add beef, eggplant (aubergines), bamboo shoots, lime leaves, sugar, coconut milk and fish sauce, cover and simmer for 35-40 minutes or until beef is tender. Stir in coriander (cilantro) and chillies.

   Note: In Thailand curries are usually served over moulds of rice. The rice absorbs and is flavoured by the large proportion of liquid in the curry. The fragrant rices such as jasmine and basmati are perfect accompaniments for Thai curries.

Serves 4

PORK AND PINEAPPLE WITH BASIL

Ingredients

4 red or golden shallots, chopped
2 fresh red chillies, finely chopped
3cm/1 1/4inch piece fresh galangal or ginger, finely chopped, or 5 slices bottled galangal, chopped
4 kaffir lime leaves
1 stalk fresh lemon grass, tender white part only, finely sliced, or 1/2 teaspoon dried lemon grass, soaked in hot water until soft
1 tablespoon tamarind concentrate
2 tablespoons lime juice
1 tablespoon water
2 teaspoons (prawn) shrimp paste
1 tablespoon dried (prawns) shrimps
350g/11oz pork fillets, cut into 3cm/1 1/4inch cubes
1 tablespoon vegetable oil
1 teaspoon palm or brown sugar
1 1/2 cups/375mL/12fl oz coconut cream
1/2 cup/125mL/4fl oz coconut milk
2 tablespoons Thai fish sauce (nam pla)
1/2 small about 200g/6 1/2oz fresh pineapple, cut into 2cm/3/4inch wide strips
60g/2oz fresh basil leaves

Method

1. Place shallots, chillies, galangal (or ginger), lime leaves, lemon grass, tamarind, 1 tablespoon lime juice, water, prawn (shrimp) paste and dried prawns (shrimps) in a food processor and process to make a thick paste, adding a little more water if necessary.
2. Place pork in a bowl, add spice paste and toss to coat pork well.
3. Heat oil in a wok or large saucepan over a medium heat, add pork and stir-fry for 5 minutes or until fragrant and pork is just cooked.
4. Stir in sugar, coconut cream and milk and fish sauce and simmer, uncovered, for 8-10 minutes or until pork is tender.
5. Add pineapple and remaining lime juice and simmer for 3 minutes or until pineapple is heated. Stir in basil.

   Note: When handling fresh chillies, do not put your hands near your eyes or allow them to touch your lips. To avoid discomfort and burning, you might like to wear gloves. Chillies are also available minced in jars from supermarkets.

Serves 4

seafood

FAVOURITE FISH

From Southern Thailand's fishing villages, boats depart at night to spotlight for squid. According to the men who work the boats, squid play games with lights and scenes are like a sea-based, strobe-lit disco. But the game-victors are the fishermen. Fresh squid is in the markets early each morning and the remainder is already on racks to dry to become one of Thailand's greatest delicacies, to be crunched on as a snack or added to seafood and fish recipes.

Suitable for Thai dishes are flounder, catfish, herring, grey and red mullet, sardines, turbot, small cod, pomfret, trout, sea bass, mackerel, plaice, sole, whiting, shark, perch, tuna, snapper and whitebait and, of course, all seafood from clams to crab. Seafood is super in a stir-fry. Prawn satays defy superlatives. Almost all fish can be grilled. Little fish deep fry well. Flavors of fragrant fish are maintained through steaming.

The oilier the fish, for example mackerel and sardines, the heavier and spicier should be the sauce. Fish and seafood are unusual for westerners to include in a salad. Results will draw many compliments to the cook.

SWEET AND SOUR FISH

Ingredients

1 whole fish, snapper or bream, about 1 1/4kg/2 1/4 lb
1/4 cup/30g/1oz flour
1 tablespoon dried chilli flakes
vegetable oil for frying

Sweet and Sour Sauce

2 cloves garlic, chopped
1 onion, chopped
1 tomato, chopped
1 carrot, sliced
2cm/3/4in cube fresh ginger, peeled
1/4 cup/60g/2oz brown sugar, well packed
2 tablespoons fish sauce
1/4 cup/60mL/2fl oz white vinegar
2 teaspoons cornflour
1/3 cup/80mL/2 1/2 fl oz water

Method

1. Clean and scale fish and wash well. Pat dry with absorbent paper. Make about 4 diagonal cuts on each side of the fish down to the bone. Coat lightly in flour and chilli flakes, shaking off any excess.
2. Heat oil in a wok or frying pan and deep-fry the fish until golden brown and crisp on both sides. Drain on absorbent paper and keep warm.
3. **Sweet and Sour Sauce:** Pour most of oil from pan, leaving 2 tablespoons and heat. Add garlic and onion and fry for 2 minutes. Stir in remaining vegetables and ginger, brown sugar, fish sauce and vinegar.
4. Mix together cornflour and water, add to pan and continue stirring until sauce boils and thickens. Lower heat and simmer until vegetables are tender but still crunchy, about 2 minutes. Serve sauce spooned over fish.

Serves 4

FISH STEW WITH LEMON GRASS AND COCONUT MILK

Ingredients

3 stalks lemon grass
2 tbsp groundnut or sesame oil
2 green chillies, deseeded and sliced
4 cloves garlic, thinly sliced
200g/7oz carrots, thinly sliced
300mL/10 fl oz fish stock
420mL/14fl oz can coconut milk
500g/1lb raw peeled tiger prawns (shrimp)
420g/14oz monkfish, cut into bite-size pieces
bunch of spring onions, shredded
200g/7oz scallops
grated rind and juice of 1 lime
fresh snipped chives to garnish
Serves 6

Method

1. Peel the outer covering from the lemon grass stalks. Finely chop the lower white bulbous parts and discard the fibrous tops. Heat the oil in a large, heavy-based saucepan, then add the chillies and lemon grass and fry for 1 minute.
2. Add garlic and carrots and fry for 3-4 minutes, until the garlic starts to turn golden. Stir in the stock and coconut milk and bring to the boil, then reduce the heat and simmer, uncovered, for 15 minutes or until reduced slightly.
3. Meanwhile, slit open the back of each prawn (shrimp) and scrape out any black vein with a small knife. Add the monkfish to coconut milk mixture, then cover and simmer for 4-5 minutes, until fish has started to turn opaque.
   Add spring onions, scallops and prawns (shrimp) and cook for 3-4 minutes, until prawns (shrimp) have turned pink and the scallops are tender and cooked through. Stir in the lime rind and juice, then sprinkle with chives.

SHELLFISH IN LEMONGRASS

Ingredients

5 red or golden shallots, chopped
4 stalks fresh lemon grass, bruised and cut into 3cm/1 1/4 in pieces, or 2 teaspoons dried lemon grass, soaked in hot water until soft
3 cloves garlic, chopped
5cm/2in piece fresh ginger, shredded
3 fresh red chillies, seeded and chopped
8 kaffir lime leaves, torn into pieces
750g/1 1/2lb mussels, scrubbed and beards removed
1/4 cup/60mL/2fl oz water
12 scallops on shells, cleaned
1 tablespoon lime juice
1 tablespoon Thai fish sauce (nam pla)
3 tablespoons fresh basil leaves

Method

1. Place shallots, lemon grass, garlic, ginger, chillies and lime leaves in a small bowl and mix to combine.
2. Place mussels in a wok and sprinkle over half the shallot mixture. Pour in water, cover and cook over a high heat for 5 minutes.
3. Add scallops, remaining shallot mixture, lime juice, fish sauce and basil and toss to combine. Cover and cook for 4-5 minutes or until mussels and scallops are cooked. Discard any mussels that do not open after 5 minutes.

Note: Serve this dish at the table straight from the wok and don't forget to give each diner some of the delicious cooking juices.

Serves 4

PRAWN (SHRIMP) AND PAW PAW SALAD

Ingredients

2 teaspoons vegetable oil
2 teaspoons chilli paste (sambal oelek)
2 stalks fresh lemon grass, chopped, or 1 teaspoon dried lemon grass, soaked in hot water until soft
2 tablespoons shredded fresh ginger
500g/1 lb medium uncooked prawns (shrimp), shelled and deveined
$^1/_2$ Chinese cabbage, shredded
4 red or golden shallots, chopped
1 pawpaw, peeled and sliced
60g/2oz watercress leaves
60g/2oz chopped roasted peanuts
30g/1oz fresh coriander (cilantro) leaves

Lime and coconut dressing

1 teaspoon brown sugar
3 tablespoons lime juice
2 tablespoons Thai fish sauce (nam pla)
1 tablespoon coconut vinegar

Method

1. Heat oil in a frying pan over a high heat, add chilli paste (sambal oelek), lemon grass and ginger and stir-fry for 1 minute. Add prawns (shrimp) and stir-fry for 2 minutes or until prawns (shrimp) change colour and are cooked through. Set aside to cool.
2. Arrange cabbage, shallots, pawpaw, watercress, peanuts, coriander (cilantro) and prawn (shrimp) mixture attractively on a serving platter.
3. To make dressing, place sugar, lime juice, fish sauce and vinegar in a bowl and mix to combine. Drizzle dressing over salad and serve.

   Note: Chinese cabbage is delicately flavoured with broad leaves and a closely packed head.

Serves 4

FISH IN GREEN MANGO SAUCE

Ingredients

4 x 185g/6oz firm fish fillets or cutlets
4 pieces banana leaf, blanched
3 cloves garlic, sliced
1 tablespoon shredded fresh ginger
2 kaffir lime leaves, shredded

Green mango sauce

1/2 small green unripe mango, flesh grated
3 red or golden shallots, chopped
2 fresh red chillies, sliced
1 tablespoon brown sugar
1/4 cup/60mL/2fl oz water
1 tablespoon Thai fish sauce (nam pla)

Method

1. Place a fish fillet or cutlet in the centre of each banana leaf. Top fish with a little each of the garlic, ginger and lime leaves, then fold over banana leaves to enclose.
2. Place parcels over a charcoal barbecue or bake in the oven for 15-20 minutes or until fish flakes when tested with a fork.
3. *To make sauce:* place mango, shallots, chillies, sugar, water and fish sauce in a saucepan and cook, stirring, over a low heat for 4-5 minutes or until sauce is heated through.
4. To serve, place parcels on serving plates, cut open to expose fish and serve with sauce.

   Note: Banana leaves are used in South-East Asian and Pacific countries in much the same way as Westerners use aluminium foil. Foil can be used if banana leaves are unavailable, however the finished dish will not have the flavour that the banana leaf contributes and it may be slightly drier.

   Oven temperature 180°C/350°F/Gas 4

Serves 4

LEMON GRASS IN TUNA

Ingredients

250g/8oz fresh egg noodles
1 tablespoon peanut (groundnut) oil
1 teaspoon sesame oil
1 onion, cut into eighths
1 tablespoon finely grated fresh ginger
2 stalks fresh lemon grass, finely chopped or 1 teaspoon dried lemon grass, soaked in hot water until soft
1 small fresh red chilli, finely chopped
3 tuna steaks, cut into thick strips
250g/8oz asparagus, cut into 5cm/2in lengths
1 red capsicum (pepper), chopped
125g/4oz snow peas (mangetout)
freshly ground black pepper
2 tablespoons flaked almonds, toasted

Basil and coconut sauce

2 tablespoons chopped fresh basil
$^1/_2$ cup/125mL/4fl oz coconut milk
1 tablespoon fish sauce
1 tablespoon sweet chilli sauce
1 tablespoon lime juice

Serves 4

Method

1. Cook noodles in boiling water in a saucepan following packet directions. Drain, set aside and keep warm.
2. To make sauce, place basil, coconut milk, fish and chilli sauces and lime juice in a bowl and mix to combine. Set aside.
3. Heat peanut (groundnut) and sesame oils together in a wok over a medium heat, add onion, ginger, lemon grass and chilli and stir-fry for 3 minutes or until onion is golden. Add tuna and stir-fry for 3 minutes or until it just changes colour. Remove mixture from wok, set aside and keep warm.
4. Add asparagus, red capsicum (pepper) and snow peas (mangetout) to wok and stir-fry for 3 minutes or until vegetables are just tender. Return tuna mixture to wok, stir in sauce and bring to the boil. Reduce heat and simmer for 3 minutes or until sauce thickens slightly. Season to taste with black pepper.
5. Divide noodles between serving plates, top with tuna mixture and scatter with almonds.

Note: If using dried lemon grass soak it in hot water for 20 minutes or until soft before using.

THAI GARLIC PRAWNS (SHRIMP)

Ingredients

6 cloves garlic, crushed
6 tablespoons chopped fresh coriander (cilantro)
3 tablespoons vegetable oil
500g/1lb uncooked large prawns (shrimp) shelled, deveined, tails left intact
3/4 cup/185mL/6fl oz water
1/4 cup/60mL/2fl oz fish sauce
1 tablespoon sugar
freshly ground black pepper

Method

1. Place garlic, coriander (cilantro) and 2 tablespoons oil in a food processor or blender and process until smooth.
2. Heat remaining oil in a large wok or frying pan, add garlic mixture and stir-fry for 2 minutes. Add prawns (shrimp) and stir-fry to coat with garlic mixture. Stir in water, fish sauce, sugar and black pepper to taste and stir-fry until prawns (shrimp) are cooked.

   Note: Fish sauce is an essential ingredient in the cuisines of Thailand, Vietnam, the Philippines and southern China. It is made from salted fish or prawns (shrimp) and is a thin brown liquid with a salty taste.

Serves 4

SOUR PRAWN (SHRIMP) CURRY

Ingredients

2 cups/500mL/16fl oz coconut milk
1 teaspoon shrimp paste
2 tablespoons Thai Green Curry Paste (see page 78)
1 stalk fresh lemon grass, finely chopped or 1/2 teaspoon dried lemon grass, soaked in hot water until soft
2 fresh green chillies, chopped
1 tablespoon ground cumin
1 tablespoon ground coriander (cilantro)
500g/1 lb uncooked large prawns, (shrimp) shelled and deveined
3 cucumbers, halved and sliced
125g/4oz canned bamboo shoots, drained
1 tablespoon tamarind concentrate, dissolved in 3 tablespoons hot water

Method

1. Place coconut milk, shrimp paste, curry paste, lemon grass, chillies, cumin and coriander (cilantro) in a wok and bring to simmering over a medium heat. Simmer, stirring occasionally, for 10 minutes.
2. Stir prawns (shrimp), cucumbers, bamboo shoots and tamarind mixture into coconut milk mixture and cook, stirring occasionally, for 10 minutes or until prawns (shrimp) are cooked.

Note: Shrimp paste is a pungent ingredient available from Oriental food shops and some supermarkets. It is made by pounding dried salted shrimp to a paste. Do not be put off by the odour of this paste as it disappears when cooked with other ingredients.

Serves 4

MUSSELS IN COCONUT VINEGAR

Ingredients

$1^1/_2$kg/3 lb mussels in their shells
6 whole coriander (cilantro) plants, washed and roughly chopped
3 stalks fresh lemon grass, bruised, or $1^1/_2$ teaspoons dried lemon grass, soaked in hot water until soft
5cm/2in piece fresh ginger, shredded
$^1/_2$ cup/125mL/4fl oz water
1 tablespoon vegetable oil
1 red onion, halved and sliced
2 fresh red chillies, sliced
2 tablespoons coconut vinegar
fresh coriander (cilantro) leaves

Method

1. Place mussels, coriander (cilantro), lemon grass, ginger and water in a wok over a high heat. Cover, cook for 5 minutes or until mussels open. Discard any mussels that do not open after 5 minutes cooking. Remove mussels from wok, discard coriander, lemon grass and ginger. Strain cooking liquid and reserve.
2. Heat oil in a wok over a medium heat, add onion and chillies and stir-fry for 3 minutes or until onion is soft. Add mussels, reserved cooking liquid and coconut vinegar and stir-fry for 2 minutes or until mussels are heated. Scatter with coriander (cilantro) leaves and serve.

   Note: This dish is delicious served with boiled egg noodles and topped with coriander (cilantro) leaves and wok juices. Coconut vinegar is made from the sap of the coconut palm. It is available from Oriental food shops. If unavailable any mild vinegar can be used instead.

Serves 4

INDIVIDUAL STEAMED FISH CURRIES

Ingredients

500g/1 lb boneless white fish fillets, cut into thin strips
1 tablespoon Thai fish sauce (nam pla)
2 tablespoons Thai Red Curry Paste (see page 78)
1 tablespoon finely grated fresh ginger
1 tablespoon finely grated lime rind
1 egg, lightly beaten
$1\frac{1}{2}$ cups/375mL/12fl oz coconut milk
3 Chinese cabbage leaves, finely shredded
2 spring onions, chopped
1 small fresh red chilli, finely sliced
2 tablespoons fresh coriander (cilantro) leaves

Method

1. Place fish, fish sauce, curry paste, ginger and lime rind into a bowl and mix to combine.
2. Place egg and coconut milk in a separate bowl and whisk to combine. Add coconut milk mixture to fish mixture and mix to combine.
3. Line four lightly greased heatproof dishes with shredded cabbage, top with fish mixture and sprinkle with spring onions, chilli and coriander (cilantro) leaves. Cover dishes with aluminium foil, place in bamboo steamer, set over a saucepan of simmering water and steam for 20 minutes or until fish is cooked.

   Note: Traditionally a Thai meal is accompanied by iced water or weak iced tea.

Serves 4

GREEN MANGO AND FISH CURRY

Ingredients

1½ cups/375mL/12fl oz coconut cream
1 teaspoon Thai Green Curry Paste (see page 78)
1 stalk fresh lemon grass, bruised, or ½ teaspoon dried lemon grass, soaked in hot water until soft
4 kaffir lime leaves, finely sliced
1 large green (unripe) mango, cut into 5mm/¼in thick slices
500g/1 lb firm fish fillets, cut into 5cm/2in cubes
1 tablespoon palm or brown sugar
2 tablespoons Thai fish sauce (nam pla)
1 tablespoon coconut vinegar
60g/2oz fresh coriander (cilantro) leaves

Method

1. Place coconut cream, curry paste, lemon grass and lime leaves in a saucepan and bring to the boil, reduce heat and simmer for 5 minutes or until fragrant.
2. Add mango and simmer for 3 minutes. Add fish, sugar and fish sauce and simmer for 3-4 minutes or until fish is cooked. Stir in vinegar and coriander (cilantro).

Note: Green (unripe) mango and pawpaw are commonly used in Thai cooking, they add a tartness to the finished dish. If green (unripe) mangoes are unavailable, use very tart green apples, but on no account use ripe mangoes as they do not give the same flavour or texture.

Serves 4

STEAMED FISH MOUSSE

Ingredients

banana leaves, blanched
2 cups/500mL/16fl oz coconut milk
3 tablespoons Thai Red Curry Paste (see page 78)
2 eggs, lightly beaten
500g/1 lb firm white fish fillets, chopped
2 kaffir lime leaves, shredded
1 teaspoon sugar
2 tablespoons Thai fish sauce (nam pla)
125g/4oz fresh basil leaves
1/2 cup/125mL/4fl oz coconut cream

Method

1. Cut six 20cm/8in circles from the banana leaves. Make four pinch pleats around the edge of the circle and secure with a toothpick to make a cup. Set aside.
2. Place 1 cup/250mL/8fl oz coconut milk in a saucepan and bring to the boil. Stir in curry paste and mix to combine.
   Remove from heat, cool slightly, then whisk in eggs. Add fish, lime leaves, sugar, fish sauce and remaining coconut milk and cook, stirring, over a low heat for 5 minutes.
3. Sprinkle the base of banana leaf cups with basil, then divide fish mixture evenly between cups. Place cups in a bamboo steamer and set aside.
4. Half fill a wok with hot water and bring to the boil. Place steamer on a wire rack in wok, cover and steam for 15 minutes. Top each mousse with a little coconut cream, then steam for 5-7 minutes longer or until mousse are firm.
   Note: If banana leaves are not available 1 cup/250mL/8fl oz capacity ramekins can be used instead.

Serves 6

FISH WITH LIME AND GARLIC

Ingredients
750g/1 1/2 lb whole fish such as sea perch, sea bass, coral trout or snapper, cleaned
2 stalks fresh lemon grass, chopped,
or 1 teaspoon dried lemon grass, soaked in hot water until soft
4 slices fresh ginger
1 fresh green chilli, halved
4 kaffir lime leaves, crushed
8 whole fresh coriander (cilantro) plants

Lime and garlic sauce
2 fresh red chillies, seeded and chopped
2 green chillies, seeded and chopped
3 cloves garlic, chopped
1 tablespoon shredded fresh ginger
1 cup/250mL/8fl oz fish or chicken stock
4 tablespoons lime juice
1 tablespoon Thai fish sauce (nam pla)

Method
1. Cut deep diagonal slits in both sides of the fish. Place lemon grass, ginger, the halved green chilli, lime leaves and coriander (cilantro) plants in cavity of fish.
2. Half fill a wok with hot water and bring to the boil. Place fish on a wire rack and place above water. Cover wok and steam for 10-15 minutes or until flesh flakes when tested with a fork.
3. To make sauce, place red and green chillies, garlic, ginger, stock, lime juice and fish sauce in a small saucepan, bring to simmering over a low heat and simmer for 4 minutes. To serve, place fish on a serving plate and spoon over sauce.

Serves 4

BARBECUED SQUID SALAD

Ingredients
1 tablespoon chilli oil
1 tablespoon finely grated lemon rind
2 teaspoons crushed black peppercorns
500g/1 lb small squid (calamari) hoods, cleaned
30g/1oz fresh basil leaves
30g/1oz fresh mint leaves
30 g/1oz fresh coriander (cilantro) leaves

Lemon and chilli dressing
1 fresh green chilli, chopped
2 tablespoons brown sugar
3 tablespoons lemon juice
2 tablespoons light soy sauce

Method
1. Place oil, lemon rind and peppercorns in a shallow dish and mix to combine. Add squid (calamari) and marinate for 30 minutes.
2. Line a serving platter with the basil, mint and coriander (cilantro). Cover with plastic food wrap and refrigerate until ready to serve.
3. To make dressing, place chilli, sugar, lemon juice and soy sauce in a bowl and mix to combine.
4. Preheat a barbecue, char-grill pan or frying pan and cook squid (calamari) for 30 seconds each side or until tender – take care not to overcook or the squid (calamari) will become tough. Place squid (calamari) on top of herbs and drizzle with dressing.

   Note: To clean squid (calamari), pull tentacles from the squid (calamari), carefully taking with them the stomach and ink bag. Next cut the beak, stomach and ink bag from the tentacles and discard. Wash tentacles well. Wash 'hood' and peel away skin. For this recipe, the hoods are left whole, if you wish the tentacles can be cut into small pieces and also used.

Serves 4

chicken & poultry

Lovers of chicken and other poultry in Thailand have an advantage over westerners fed on battery hens, so processed to maintain demand and supposedly cost-efficient. Almost all Thai poultry is free-range and more flavorsome. Indeed, one wonders how, around proud, ancient ruins in the shadows of giant Buddha statues, and even remote elephant camps in Northern Thailand, magnificently feathered siring roosters, (the majority spared from cock fights), and hens, chicks, also ducks and drakes, splashing around in klongs and ponds, are recognised by their owners. Let alone how and where eggs are collected. But somehow the poultry gets to market, often live, to become a vital ingredient on the Thai menu. It can appear with rice soup breakfast and, at lunchtime in the fields, cold and smeared with chilli paste or dunked in fish sauce. It comes with Chinese-style rice or Thai noodles or wrapped with spicy sauce in pancakes. It's sassy as satay at hawkers' stalls.

Fried, stir-fried, grilled, roasted, barbecued, simmered in a soup, slow-cooked, curried, minced and stuffed into a spring roll or added to a spicy salad, steamed or boiled for its meat as well as stock, chicken is the world's most versatile and adaptable meat for innovative combo recipes. There will be no complaints, such can be the amazing variety of dishes.

THAI-SPICED CHICKEN WITH COURGETTES (ZUCCHINI)

Ingredients

1 tbsp olive oil
1 clove garlic, finely chopped
2½cm/1in fresh root ginger, finely chopped
1 small fresh red chilli, deseeded and finely chopped
350g/12oz skinless boneless chicken breasts, cut into strips
1 tbsp Thai 7-spice seasoning
1 red and 1 yellow pepper (capsicum), deseeded and sliced
2 courgettes (zucchini), thinly sliced
220g/7oz can bamboo shoots, drained
2 tbsp dry sherry or apple juice
1 tbsp light soy sauce
black pepper
2 tbsp chopped fresh coriander (cilantro), plus extra to garnish

Ingredients

1. Heat the oil in a non-stick wok or large frying pan. Add the garlic, ginger and chilli and stir-fry for 30 seconds to release the flavours.
2. Add the chicken and Thai seasoning and stir-fry for 4 minutes or until the chicken has coloured. Add the peppers (capsicum) and courgettes (zucchini) and stir-fry for 1-2 minutes, until slightly softened.
3. Stir in the bamboo shoots and stir-fry for another 2-3 minutes, until the chicken is cooked through and tender. Add the sherry or apple juice, soy sauce and black pepper and sizzle for 1-2 minutes. Remove from the heat and stir in the chopped fresh coriander (cilantro), then garnish with more coriander (cilantro).

Serves 4

THAI GREEN DUCK CURRY WITH BAMBOO SHOOTS

Ingredients

2 tbsp vegetable oil
3 tbsp Thai green curry paste
4 boneless duck breasts, skinned and cut into 2½cm/1in chunks
410mL/13oz can coconut milk
220g/7oz can sliced bamboo shoots, drained
2 tbsp Thai fish sauce
1 tsp soft dark brown sugar
salt
3 tbsp chopped fresh basil, plus extra leaves to garnish
4 tbsp chopped fresh coriander (cilantro)

Method

1. Heat the oil in a large, heavy-based saucepan, then add the curry paste and fry, stirring frequently, for 3 minutes or until the aromas are released. Add the duck, turn to coat thoroughly, then fry for 4-5 minutes, stirring from time to time.
2. Stir in the coconut milk, bamboo shoots, fish sauce, sugar and salt to taste. Bring to the boil, stirring often, then reduce the heat. Simmer, uncovered, for 30-35 minutes until the duck is tender, stirring occasionally. Just before serving, stir in the chopped basil and coriander (cilantro), and garnish with basil leaves.

Serves 4

CHICKEN AND CAPSICUM (PEPPER) SALAD

Ingredients
1 teaspoon sesame oil
1 teaspoon chilli oil
1 stalk fresh lemon grass, finely chopped or 1/2 teaspoon dried lemon grass, soaked in hot water until soft
315g/10oz lean chicken mince
185g/6oz water chestnuts, chopped
1 tablespoon soy sauce
assorted lettuce leaves
1 red capsicum (pepper), thinly sliced
1 green capsicum (pepper), thinly sliced
60g/2oz bean sprouts
1/2 cup/45g/1 1/2oz shredded coconut, toasted

Mint dressing
3 tablespoons chopped fresh mint
1 clove garlic, crushed
1 tablespoon brown sugar
1/4 cup/60mL/2fl oz water
1 tablespoon fish sauce
1 tablespoon lime juice

Method
1. Heat sesame and chilli oils together in a wok over a medium heat, add lemon grass and stir-fry for 2 minutes or until golden.
2. Add chicken, water chestnuts and soy sauce and stir-fry for 5 minutes or until chicken is tender. Remove pan from heat and cool slightly.
3. Arrange lettuce leaves on a large platter. Place chicken mixture, red capsicum (pepper), green capsicum (pepper), bean sprouts and coconut in a bowl and toss to combine. Arrange chicken mixture on lettuce.
4. To make dressing, place mint, garlic, sugar, water, fish sauce and lime juice in a bowl and mix to combine. Spoon dressing over salad and serve.
   Note: Fish sauce is a pungent Oriental ingredient that is used extensively in Thai cooking. It is available from Oriental food shops and some supermarkets.

Serves 4

CARDAMOM AND ORANGE DUCK

Ingredients

1 1/2kg/3lb Chinese barbecued or roasted duck
3 cups/750mL/1 1/4pt chicken stock
2 small fresh red chillies, halved
3cm/1 1/4in piece fresh galangal or ginger, sliced, or 5 slices bottled galangal
2 stalks fresh lemon grass, cut into 3cm/1 1/4in pieces, bruised, or 1 teaspoon dried lemon grass, soaked in hot water until soft
6 whole coriander (cilantro) plants, washed, stems and roots removed, leaves reserved
6 cardamom pods, crushed
4 kaffir lime leaves, torn into pieces
1 large orange, peeled, all white pith removed from rind, flesh segmented and reserved
1 tablespoon vegetable oil
2 teaspoons shrimp paste
2 teaspoons Thai Red Curry paste (see page 78)
1 clove garlic, finely chopped
1 tablespoon palm or brown sugar
2 spring onions, cut into thin strips

Method

1. Remove meat from duck and cut into bite-sized pieces – reserve bones, skin and as many of the juices as possible. Place reserved bones, skin and juices, stock, chillies, galangal or ginger, lemon grass, coriander (cilantro) stems and roots, cardamom pods, lime leaves and orange rind in a saucepan and bring to the boil. Reduce heat and simmer, uncovered, for 15 minutes. Strain liquid and set aside. Discard solids.
2. Heat oil in a wok or large saucepan over a medium heat, add shrimp and curry pastes and garlic and cook, stirring, for 1-2 minutes or until fragrant.
3. Add duck pieces and stir to coat with spice paste. Add reserved liquid and simmer for 3-4 minutes or until liquid reduces slightly. Stir in orange segments, coriander leaves and sugar. Serve scattered with spring onions.

Note: Chinese barbecued or roasted duck is available from Oriental food stores which sell meat. If unavailable roast duck can be used instead.

Serves 4

GREEN CHICKEN CURRY

Ingredients

1 tablespoon peanut (groundnut) oil
1 onion, chopped
1 stalk fresh lemon grass, finely chopped or 1 teaspoon dried lemon grass, soaked in hot water until soft
3 kaffir lime leaves, finely shredded
2 tablespoons Thai Green Curry Paste (see page 78)
1 teaspoon shrimp paste (optional)
2 cups/500mL/16fl oz coconut milk
1 tablespoon Thai fish sauce (nam pla)
1 tablespoon sugar
1 kg/2lb boneless chicken thigh or breast fillets, cut into 2cm/3/4in cubes
220g/7oz canned bamboo shoots, drained
315g/10oz canned baby sweet corn, drained
2 tablespoons chopped fresh basil

Method

1. Heat oil in a wok over a medium heat, add onion, lemon grass and lime leaves and stir-fry for 3 minutes or until onion is golden.
2. Add curry paste and shrimp paste (if using) and stir-fry for 3 minutes longer or until fragrant. Stir in coconut milk, fish sauce and sugar, bring to the boil, then reduce heat and simmer, stirring frequently, for 10 minutes.
3. Add chicken, bamboo shoots, sweet corn and basil and cook, stirring frequently, for 15 minutes or until chicken is tender.

   Note: Fresh lemon grass is available from Oriental food shops and some supermarkets and greengrocers. It is also available dried; if using dried lemon grass soak it in hot water for 20 minutes or until soft before using. Lemon grass is also available in bottles from supermarkets, use this in the same way as you would fresh lemon grass.

Serves 6

SPICED COCONUT CHICKEN

Ingredients

2 teaspoons vegetable oil
2 stalks fresh lemon grass, chopped or 1 teaspoon dried lemon grass soaked in hot water until soft
2 teaspoons finely grated fresh ginger
1 teaspoon ground cumin
4 boneless chicken breast fillets, cut into thick slices
3 tablespoons chopped fresh coriander (cilantro)
1 cup/250mL/8fl oz coconut milk
1/2 cup/125mL/4fl oz chicken stock
125g/4oz snowpeas, (mangetout), trimmed
freshly ground black pepper
4 tablespoons unsalted peanuts, roasted and chopped

Method

1. Heat oil in a wok over a high heat, add lemongrass, ginger and cumin and stir-fry for 1 minute. Add chicken and stir-fry for 3 minutes or until chicken is golden.
2. Stir in coriander (cilantro), coconut milk and stock, bring to boil and simmer for 5 minutes. Add snowpeas (mangetout) and cook for 1 minute or until snowpeas (mangetout) change colour. Season to taste with black pepper. Scatter with peanuts and serve.

   Note: For a complete meal, serve on a bed of fragrant rice. Jasmine or Basmati rice are both readily available from supermarkets and Oriental food stores.

Serves 4

STIRFRIED DUCK IN GREENS

Ingredients

1 kg/2lb Chinese barbecued or roasted duck
2 teaspoons vegetable oil
1 tablespoon Thai Red Curry Paste (see page 78)
1 teaspoon shrimp paste
1 stalk fresh lemon grass, finely sliced, or 1/2 teaspoon dried lemon grass, soaked in hot water until soft
4 fresh red chillies
1 bunch Chinese broccoli (gai lum) or Swiss chard, chopped
1 tablespoon palm or brown sugar
2 tablespoons tamarind concentrate
1 tablespoon Thai fish sauce (nam pla)

Method

1. Slice meat from duck, leaving the skin on, and cut into bite-sized pieces. Reserve as many of the cavity juices as possible.
2. Heat oil in a wok over a medium heat, add curry paste, shrimp paste, lemon grass and chillies and stir-fry for 3 minutes or until fragrant.
3. Add duck and reserved juices and stir-fry for 2 minutes or until coated in spice mixture and heated. Add broccoli or chard, sugar, tamarind and fish sauce and stir-fry for 3-4 minutes or until broccoli is wilted.

Note: Chinese broccoli (gai lum) is a popular Asian vegetable. It has dark green leaves on firm stalks often with small white flowers.

The leaves, stalks and flowers are all used in cooking, however the stalks are considered to be the choicest part of the plant. To prepare, remove leaves from stalks and peel, then chop both leaves and stalks and use as directed in the recipe.

Serves 4

CHICKEN PHANAENG CURRY

Ingredients

2 cups/500mL/16fl oz coconut milk
3 tablespoons Thai red curry paste
500g/1 lb chicken breast fillets, sliced
250g/8oz snake (yard-long) or green beans
3 tablespoons unsalted peanuts, roasted and finely chopped
2 teaspoons brown or palm sugar
1 tablespoon Thai fish sauce (nam pla)
1/2 cup/125mL/4fl oz coconut cream
2 tablespoons fresh basil leaves
2 tablespoons fresh coriander (cilantro) leaves
sliced fresh red chilli

Method

1. Place coconut milk in a saucepan and bring to the boil over a high heat, then boil until oil separates from coconut milk and it reduces and thickens slightly. Stir in curry paste and boil for 2 minutes or until fragrant.
2. Add chicken, beans, peanuts, sugar and fish sauce and simmer for 5-7 minutes or until chicken is tender. Stir in coconut cream, basil and coriander (cilantro). Serve garnished with slices of chilli.

Note: To store whole fresh coriander (cilantro) plants, place roots in 1cm/1/2in of water in a glass jar, cover coriander and jar with a plastic bag, secure bag around jar and store in the refrigerator. Coriander (cilantro) and other fresh herbs purchased in good condition will keep for a week or more when stored in this way. Do not wash the herbs before storing.

Serves 4

CHICKEN IN COCONUT MILK

Ingredients

1kg/2lb chicken pieces, e.g. drumsticks, thighs, half breasts
1 onion, chopped
2 cups/500mL/16fl oz coconut milk
4 dried kaffir leaves
2cm/$^3/_4$in cube fresh ginger, peeled and chopped
1 green chilli, seeded and chopped
2 tablespoons lemon juice
2 tablespoons fish sauce
2 teaspoons brown sugar
$^1/_3$ cup/60g/2oz peanuts, roughly chopped
2 tablespoons coriander (cilantro), chopped

Method

1. Remove skin form chicken pieces and discard. Place chicken pieces into a large saucepan.
2. Add all remaining ingredients and bring to the boil. Lower heat and simmer uncovered for 30-35 minutes or until chicken is cooked. Remove kaffir leaves and discard. Sprinkle with coriander (cilantro) and serve with steamed long-grain rice.

Serves 4

CHICKEN IN GARLIC PEPPER

Ingredients

4 cloves garlic
3 fresh coriander (cilantro) roots
1 tspn crushed black peppercorns
500g/1 lb chicken breast fillets chopped into 3cm/1$^1/_4$in cubes
vegetable oil for deep-frying
30g/1oz fresh basil leaves
30g/1oz fresh mint leaves
sweet chilli sauce

Method

1. Place garlic, coriander (cilantro) roots and black peppercorns in a food processor and process to make a paste. Coat chicken with garlic paste and marinate for 1 hour.
2. Heat oil in a wok or frying pan over a high heat until a cube of bread dropped in browns in 50 seconds, then deep-fry chicken, a few pieces at a time, for 2 minutes or until golden and tender. Drain on absorbent kitchen paper.
3. Deep-fry basil and mint until crisp, then drain and place on a serving plate. Top with chicken and serve with chilli sauce.
   Note: Thai cooks use three types of basil in cooking - Asian sweet, holy and lemon - each has a distinctive flavour and is used for specific types of dishes. For this dish Asian sweet basil, known in Thailand as horapa, would be used.

Serves 4

CHICKEN WITH CHILLI JAM

Ingredients

2 teaspoons vegetable oil
3 chicken breast fillets or 4 boneless thigh fillets, cut into thin strips
4 red or golden shallots, chopped
185g/6oz broccoli, chopped
125g/4oz snow peas (mangetout), halved
60g/2oz unsalted, roasted cashews
2 tablespoons light soy sauce

Chilli jam

2 teaspoons vegetable oil
4 fresh red chillies, sliced
1 tablespoon shredded fresh ginger
1 teaspoon shrimp paste
$^1/_3$ cup/90g/3oz sugar
$^1/_3$ cup/90mL/3fl oz water
2 tablespoons lime juice

Method

1. To make jam, heat oil in a wok over a medium heat, add chillies, ginger and shrimp paste and stir-fry for 1 minute or until golden. Stir in sugar, water and lime juice and cook, stirring, for 3 minutes or until mixture is thick. Remove jam from wok and set aside.
2. Heat oil in a clean wok over a high heat for 1 minute, add chicken and shallots and stir-fry for 3 minutes or until chicken is lightly browned.
3. Add broccoli, snow peas (mangetout), cashews and soy sauce and stir-fry for 3 minutes longer or until vegetables change colour and are cooked.
4. To serve, place chicken on serving plate and top with Chilli Jam.
   Note: Serve this tasty chicken dish with steamed jasmine rice. If you prefer, the Chilli Jam can be served separately so that each diner can season their serving according to individual taste.

Serves 4

rice & noodles

Rice is the staff of Thai life. Thais know if rice is young, therefore needing less cooking water than the old, which is what most westerners buy, totally dry - unless it's sold wet, meaning fresh, at an oriental store.

Opt for fragrant or long-grained, polished rice although short rice can be used if necessary. Mostly steamed, sometimes boiled, rice is also popular fried, adapted from the recipe introduced from Southern China long ago.

Unlike Italian pasta and noodles, dried Asian noodles are quick cooking, usually two minutes at the most. The time catch is in peeling, chopping or par-cooking other ingredients but even fumble-fingered westerners can become adept with practice.

Nam Prik sauce, mentioned on page 12, is one essential dipping sauce hotly enhancing any finished noodle dish or plain rice. You'll serve rice with Thai food but you really cannot claim to having eaten Thai cuisine unless you've gone off your noodle with delight when nourished by noodles.

CELLOPHANE NOODLE SALAD

Ingredients

155g/5oz cellophane noodles
2 teaspoons sesame oil
2 cloves garlic, crushed
1 tablespoon finely grated fresh ginger
500g/1 lb pork mince
15g/$^1/_2$oz mint leaves
15g/$^1/_2$oz coriander (cilantro) leaves
8 lettuce leaves
5 red or golden shallots, chopped
1 fresh red chilli, sliced
2 tablespoons lemon juice
1 tablespoon light soy sauce

Method

1. Place noodles in a bowl and pour over boiling water to cover. Stand for 10 minutes, then drain well.
2. Heat oil in a frying pan over a high heat, add garlic and ginger and stir-fry for 1 minute. Add pork, stir-fry for 5 minutes or until pork is browned and cooked.
3. Arrange mint, coriander (cilantro), lettuce, shallots, chilli and noodles on a serving platter. Top with pork mixture, then drizzle with lemon juice and soy sauce.

   Note: Cellophane noodles also known as glass noodles and bean thread noodles or vermicelli are made from mung bean flour and are either very thin vermicelli-style noodles or flatter fettuccine-style noodles. In the dried state they are very tough and difficult to break. For ease of use it is best to buy a brand which packages them as bundles.

Serves 4

PAD THAI WITH PORK AND PRAWNS (SHRIMP)

Ingredients

250g/8oz pack rice noodles
4 tbsp groundnut oil
2 cloves garlic, chopped
1 shallot, chopped
125g/4oz pork fillet, cut into 5mm /1/4in thick strips
1 tbsp Thai fish sauce
1 tsp sugar
juice of 1/2 lime
1 tbsp light soy sauce
1 tbsp tomato ketchup
220g/7oz pack fresh bean sprouts
125g/4oz cooked peeled prawns (shrimp), defrosted if frozen
black pepper
50g/2oz roasted salted peanuts, chopped
1 tbsp chopped fresh coriander (cilantro)
1 lime, quartered, to serve

Method

1. Prepare the rice noodles according to the packet instructions. Drain and rinse. Heat a wok, then add the oil. Stir-fry the garlic, shallot and pork for 3 minutes or until the pork turns opaque. Stir in the rice noodles and mix thoroughly.
2. Mix together the fish sauce, sugar, lime juice, soy sauce and ketchup, then add to the noodle mixture, stirring well. Stir-fry for 5 minutes. Mix in the bean sprouts and prawns (shrimp) and stir-fry for a further 5 minutes or until the bean sprouts are tender. Season with black pepper.
3. Transfer the mixture to a serving dish. Sprinkle over the peanuts and coriander (cilantro), then serve with lime wedges. Serve 4

STEAMED RICE IN BANANA LEAVES

Ingredients

2 cups/440g/14oz long grain white glutinous rice, soaked overnight
1 cup/250mL/8fl oz coconut cream
4x30cm/12in squares banana leaf or aluminium foil
220g/7oz boneless chicken breast fillet,sliced
4 red or goldern shallots, chopped
3 fresh red chillies, chopped
2 tablespoons finely grated fresh ginger

Method

1. Drain rice, place in a colander and rinse under cold running water until water runs clear. Place rice in a saucepan and pour over enough water to just cover. Cover pan with a tight-fitting lid and cook over a medium-low heat for 20 minutes or until water is absorbed.
2. Transfer rice to a bowl and fluff up with a fork. Stir in coconut cream and stand for 10 minutes.
3. Divide half the rice between the banana leaves or aluminium foil squares. Spread rice out evenly, then top with chicken, shallots, chillies and ginger. Cover with remaining rice and fold banana leaf or aluminium foil to enclose.
4. Half fill a wok with water and bring to the boil. Place parcels in a bamboo steamer. Place steamer on a wire rack in wok, cover steamer and steam for 10 minutes.

Note: White glutinous rice can either be long or short grained and is sometimes called sweet or sticky rice. For savoury dishes such as this one, Thai cooks would use the long grain variety. Glutinous rice has a very high starch content, the cooked grains cling together in a mass and are soft and sticky. Short grain white glutinous rice is mainly used in sweets. You can also get a black glutinous rice.

Serves 4

NOODLES WITH VEGETABLE AND OYSTER SAUCE

Ingredients

200g/7oz Chinese egg noodles
4 Chinese dried mushrooms
1 tablespoon oil
3 cloves garlic, chopped
1-2 red chillies, finely chopped
6 shallots, sliced
2 sticks celery, sliced
1 red capsicum (pepper), sliced
2 cups/125g/4oz shredded cabbage
3 tablespoons oyster sauce
1 tablespoon fish sauce
1 tablespoon brown sugar
2 tablespoons water
1/4 cup/45g/1 1/2oz chopped peanuts

Method

1. Cook egg noodles in a large saucepan of boiling water until tender, about 5 minutes. Drain well. Soak mushrooms in hot water for 20 minutes, then slice thinly.
2. Heat oil in a wok or large frying pan, add garlic and chillies and fry for 1 minutes.
3. Add all other ingredients except peanuts and noodles, bring to the boil. Lower heat and simmer for 2 minutes or until vegetables are tender but still crunchy.
4. Stir in cooked noodles and heat for 1 minute or until noodles are heated through. Serve sprinkled with peanuts.

Serves 6

THAI FRIED RICE

Ingredients

2 tablespoons oil
4 cloves garlic, crushed
400g/13oz lean pork, chopped
2 red or green capsicums (peppers), chopped
4 spring onions, chopped
4 tablespoons fish sauce
4 tablespoons tomato sauce
375g/12oz cooked prawns (shrimp), peeled
8 cups/1 1/2kg/3lb cooked long-grain rice
2 eggs, lightly beaten

Method

1. Heat oil in a large frying pan. Add garlic and pork and fry until pork is golden brown.
2. Add capsicum (pepper), spring onions, fish sauce, tomato sauce, prawns (shrimp) and rice, cook over a moderate heat for 3 minutes.
3. Stir in beaten eggs and mix lightly through. Cover with a lid and cook for 2-3 minutes, stirring once or twice
   Note: This fried rice is great when entertaining a crowd.
   It serves 8 as a main meal or 10-12 with other dishes at a party. The recipe is easily doubled or halved.

Serves 8

RICE NOODLES IN GREENS

Ingredients

350g/11oz thick fresh or dried rice noodles
1 tablespoon vegetable oil
2 tablespoons shredded fresh ginger
2 cloves garlic, crushed
250g/8oz Chinese broccoli (gai lum), chopped
125g/4oz asparagus, cut in half
3 tablespoons snipped fresh garlic chives
1/3 cup/90mL/3fl oz vegetable stock
2 tablespoons light soy sauce
1 teaspoon cornflour blended with
2 teaspoons water

Method

1. Place noodles in a bowl and pour over boiling water to cover. If using fresh noodles soak for 2 minutes; if using dried noodles soak for 5-6 minutes or until soft. Drain well and set aside.
2. Heat oil in a wok or frying pan over a medium heat, add ginger and garlic and stir-fry for 1 minute. Add broccoli, asparagus, chives, stock and soy sauce and stir-fry for 2 minutes.
3. Add noodles to wok and stir-fry for 4 minutes or until heated through. Stir in cornflour mixture and cook for 1 minute or until mixture thickens.

Serves 4

FISH AND RICE NOODLES

Ingredients

1 teaspoon sesame oil
1 teaspoon vegetable oil
1 stalk fresh lemon grass, chopped or 1/2 teaspoon dried lemon grass soaked in hot water until soft
500g/1 lb ocean trout or salmon fillets, bones and skin removed, cut into 2cm/3/4 in thick strips
2 tablespoons chopped fresh coriander (cilantro)
2 tablespoons lime juice
250g/8oz asparagus, chopped
185g/6oz broccoli, chopped
3 tablespoons sweet chilli sauce
2 tablespoons reduced-salt soy sauce
500g/1 lb fresh rice noodles

Method

1. Heat sesame and vegetable oils together in a wok over a medium heat, add lemon grass and stir-fry for 1 minute. Add fish, coriander (cilantro) and lime juice and stir-fry for 1 minute or until fish is golden. Remove fish mixture from wok and set aside.
2. Add asparagus, broccoli and chilli and soy sauces to wok and stir-fry for 2 minutes. Add noodles and gently stir-fry for 2 minutes longer, then return fish mixture to pan and cook for 1 minute or until heated through. Serve immediately.
   Note: Fresh rice noodles are lightly cooked soft, wet noodles made from a sweet glutinous rice. Take care when cooking the noodles as they are delicate and can easily be overcooked.

Serves 4

desserts

So richly endowed with fruits, cold-climate in the north and tropical in the central plains and south, Thai cooks never need to wonder what to serve as dessert to finish off a wonderful meal. Fruit is selected, not just because of its availability, but because it is a coolant after the hot and spicy dishes which may have preceded the last course. Dessert is the only course which is served separately in Thailand.

Fruit is fabulous, even if it hasn't been grown in the region where it will be eaten. Trucks, their loads well covered to protect them from fumes and dust, make hair-raising dashes from north to south and vice versa. They arrive at markets in time to convince discerning buyers the produce is fresh. This means almost every part of Thailand offers all conceivable fruits in season.

The Thais don't dominate their menus with desserts and time is always a constraint - maybe after hours of pre-preparing their mains. A fancy, layered sponge may crown the table. Bangkok, in particular, has many patisseries from which people buy magnificently decorated cakes (with false cream), for special occasions. Many western cooks can whip up a sponge effortlessly. It can substitute for a Thai dessert - and be filled with fresh cream. Ensure your table is decorated with fresh flowers or leaves.

ORIENTAL FRUIT SALAD

Ingredients

3 stalks lemon grass
50g/2oz caster sugar
1 small cantaloupe melon
1 mango
440g/14oz can lychees, drained
fresh mint leaves to garnish

Method

1. Peel the outer layers from the lemon grass stalks, finely chop the lower white bulbous parts and discard the fibrous tops. Place the lemon grass, sugar and 100mL/4fl oz of water in a saucepan. Simmer, stirring, for 5 minutes or until the sugar dissolves, then bring to the boil. Remove from the heat and leave to cool for 20 minutes. Refrigerate for 30 minutes.
2. Halve the melon and scrape out the seeds. Cut into wedges, then remove the skin and cut the flesh into small chunks. Slice off the two fat sides of the mango close to the stone. Cut a criss-cross pattern across the flesh (but not the skin) of each piece, then push the skin inside out to expose the cubes of flesh and cut them off.
3. Place the melon, mango and lychees in serving bowls. Strain the lemon grass syrup and pour over the fruit. Decorate with mint.

   Note: If you're serving a very spicy or rich meal, give your guests this light and unusual fruit salad to finish.

Serves 4

BAKED PASSION FRUIT CUSTARDS

Ingredients

4 large eggs, beaten
4 tbsp caster sugar
155mL/5fl oz coconut milk
pinch of salt
2 passion fruit

Method

1. Preheat the oven to 180°C/350°F/Gas 4. Whisk together the eggs, sugar, coconut milk and salt until smooth, then pour into 4 ramekins.
2. Halve 1 passion fruit, scoop out the pulp and seeds and divide between the 4 custard-filled ramekins. Place them in a deep roasting tin.
3. Pour boiling water into the roasting tin to come three-quarters of the way up the sides of the ramekins. Bake the custards for 40 minutes. Serve warm or cold with the pulp and seeds from the remaining passion fruit spooned over the top.

Note: This creamy dessert is totally delicious. The passion fruit gives the custard a distinctive sweetness and the seeds add texture, but you can use fresh mango if you prefer.

Serves 4

BANANA FRITTERS

Ingredients
4 large firm bananas, cut in half then split lengthways
2 tablespoons lime juice
vegetable oil for deep-frying

Batter
1 cup/125g/4oz self-raising flour
2 tablespoons caster sugar
1/2 cup/125mL/4fl oz milk
1 egg, lightly beaten
1 egg white

Caramel sauce
1/2 cup/125g/4oz brown or palm sugar
1/2 cup/125mL/4fl oz water
1/2 cup/125mL/4fl oz cream (double)
2 teaspoons whisky (optional)

Method
1. To make batter, sift flour in a bowl and make a well in the centre. Combine caster sugar, milk and egg, then mix into flour mixture to make a batter of a smooth consistency. Stand for 10 minutes.
2. To make sauce, place sugar and water in a saucepan and cook over a low heat, stirring constantly, until sugar dissolves. Bring to the boil, then reduce heat and simmer, without stirring, for 5 minutes or until mixture is golden.
3. Remove pan from heat and carefully stir in cream and whisky, if using. Return pan to a low heat and cook, stirring, until combined. Cool.
4. Beat egg white until soft peaks form, then fold into batter. Heat oil in a saucepan until a cube of bread dropped in browns in 50 seconds. Brush bananas with lime juice,dip in batter to coat then drain off excess. Cook bananas in hot oil for 2-3 minutes or until golden. Serve immediately with sauce.

Serves 4

MANGO ICE CREAM

Ingredients

8 egg yolks
$1^1/_4$ cups/280g/9oz caster sugar
4 cups/1 litre/$1^3/_4$ pt milk
2 cups/500mL/16fl oz cream (double)
2 teaspoons vanilla essence
250g/8oz mango, puréed

Method

1. Place egg yolks and sugar in a mixing bowl and beat until thick and creamy.
2. Place milk and cream in a large saucepan and bring just to the boil. Remove from heat and whisk gradually into egg yolk mixture. Return to pan and cook over a low heat, stirring constantly, until mixture coats the back of a wooden spoon.
3. Stir in vanilla essence and fold in mango purée. Transfer mixture to an ice cream maker and freeze according to the manufacturer's instructions.

Cook's tip: If you do not have an ice cream maker, place the custard mixture in a deep-sided metal container and freeze until the mixture begins to set around the edge. Then remove from freezer and beat with an electric mixer until smooth. To ensure a smooth texture, repeat this process 2-3 times more to prevent large ice crystals forming.

Makes $1^1/_2$ litres/$2^1/_2$pt

Banana leaves: Before using fresh banana leaves for wrapping food they need to be softened. This can be done by: passing the leaves over a gas flame until they are soft; blanching in boiling water for 20-30 seconds; or heating in the microwave on HIGH (100%) for 45-60 seconds or until soft. Remove the thick mid-rib before using or the leaves will be difficult to wrap around the food.

Basil: Thai cooks use three main types of basil in cooking. Asian sweet or cinnamon basil, known in Thailand as horapa, is usually added at the end of cooking to give a final aromatic fragrance to the food. Holy basil, known as kaprao, is used in strongly flavoured dishes and is cooked in the dishes to impart its flavour. Lemon basil, known as manglak, as the name suggests has a lemon scent. It is mainly used in soups and sprinkled over salads. Ordinary basil can be used in place of any of the above. In this book the recipes do not specify which type of basil to use, but for an authentic Thai flavour choose the appropriate basil as discussed above.

Bitter melon (gourd): This cucumber-like melon has a lumpy skin and as the name suggests has a bitter taste. To use, peel, remove seeds and cut into cubes, strips or thin slices, then degorge by sprinkling with salt and allowing to stand for about 1 hour. Rinse under cold water and drain well. The degorging reduces bitterness, but to further reduce bitterness the melon can also be blanched in boiling water for a few minutes.

Coconut milk/cream: Coconut milk and coconut cream are essentially the same product. Coconut cream is very thick coconut milk and is the result of the first pressing of the coconut flesh. Coconut milk can be purchased in a number of forms – canned, as a long-life product in cartons or as a powder to which your add water. Once opened, it has a short life and should be used within a day or so.

You can make coconut milk using desiccated coconut and water. To make coconut milk, place 500 g/1 lb desiccated coconut in a bowl and pour over 3 cups/750 mL/1 1/4pt boiling water. Leave to stand for 30 minutes, then strain, squeezing the coconut to extract as much liquid as possible. This will make a thick coconut milk or what is referred to in this book as coconut cream. The coconut can be used again to make a thinner coconut milk, the product referred to as coconut milk in this book.

Coconut vinegar: Made from the sap of the coconut palm, coconut vinegar is available from Oriental food shops. If unavailable, any mild vinegar can be used.

Coriander (cilantro): The leaves, seeds and roots of this plant are used in Thai cooking. It is considered to be essential to Thai cuisine and almost every dish is garnished with fresh coriander leaves. The three parts of the plant all have a distinctively different flavour and one should not be substituted for another.

CURRY PASTES

Curry pastes are readily available from supermarkets and Oriental food shops. Homemade curry pastes are easy to make and will keep for about a week if stored in an airtight container in the refrigerator.

Thai Green Curry Paste: Chop 6 spring onions, 8 fresh green chillies, 4 cloves garlic and 2 stalks fresh lemon grass. Heat 1 tablespoon vegetable oil in a frying pan over a medium heat. Add spring onions, chillies, lemon grass and garlic. Cook, stirring, for 3 minutes or until soft. Cool slightly. Place garlic mixture, 1 tablespoon finely grated lime rind, 2 teaspoons lime juice, 2 tablespoons chopped fresh coriander (cilantro) leaves, 1 tablespoon ground coriander, (cilantro) 2 teaspoons ground cumin, 1 teaspoon ground turmeric and 2 tablespoons brown sugar and 1 teaspoon shrimp paste (optional) in a food processor or blender. Process to make a smooth paste. Heat 2 tablespoons vegetable oil in a frying pan over a medium heat. Add paste. Cook, stirring constantly, for 5 minutes or until a thick paste forms. Makes 1 cup/250 mL/8 fl oz.

Thai Red Curry Paste: Chop 8 small fresh red chillies, 6 spring onions, 6 cloves garlic and 2 stalks fresh lemon grass. Heat 3 tablespoons vegetable oil in a frying pan over a medium heat. Add chillies, spring onions, garlic, lemon grass and 1 teaspoon caraway seeds. Cook, stirring, for 3 minutes or until golden. Cool slightly. Place onion mixture, 2 tablespoons ground coriander, 2 tablespoons finely grated fresh galangal (optional), 2 teaspoons Thai fish sauce (nam pla), 2 teaspoons lime juice, 2 teaspoons finely grated lime rind and 1 teaspoon shrimp paste in a food processor or blender. Shred 6 kaffir lime leaves. Add to processor.

Process to make a smooth paste. Heat 2 tablespoons vegetable oil in a frying pan over a medium heat. Add paste. Cook, stirring, for 5 minutes or until a thick paste forms. Makes 1 cup/250mL/8 fl oz

Dried (Prawns) Shrimps:
These can be purchased whole or shredded in plastic packets from Oriental food stores. If stored in the refrigerator they should last for several months. Choose prawns (shrimps) which are a salmon pink colour and slightly soft – very hard (prawn) shrimps or those that smell of ammonia should be avoided.

Galangal:
This spice belongs to the same family as ginger. In Thai cooking it is usually greater galangal that is used. Where other Asian cuisines would use ginger, Thai cooks use galangal. It can be purchased fresh or bottled in brine. Bottled galangal is more tender and not as fibrous as the fresh product and as such is somewhat easier to use. Bottled galangal will keep for months in the refrigerator. If unavailable, fresh ginger can be used instead, but will give a different flavour to the finished dish.

Kaffir limes:
Both the fruit and the leaves of this citrus tree are used in Thai cooking. Both have a distinctive flavour and perfume. The leaves are available dried, fresh frozen or fresh from Oriental food shops and some greengrocers. If kaffir lime leaves are unavailable a little finely grated lime rind can be used instead. The fruit of the kaffir lime is very dark green with a thick, bumpy and wrinkled rind. In this book we have not specified the use of kaffir limes for lime juice, but for a true Thai flavour use it whenever possible.

Lemon grass:
Fresh lemon grass is available from Oriental food shops and some supermarkets and greengrocers. It is also available dried: if using dried lemon grass, soak it in hot water for 20 minutes or until soft before using. Lemon grass can be purchased in bottles from supermarkets – use this in the same way as you would fresh lemon grass. There is also a powdered form available which is called sereh, this is strong in flavour and should be used with discretion. If lemon grass is unavailable, lemon balm, lemon verbena or lemon rind are possible substitutes.

Oriental rice paper:
This is made from a paste of ground rice and water which is stamped into rounds and dried. When moistened the brittle sheets become flexible. It is used to make delicacies such as the Herbed Vegetable Rolls on page 18. Sold in sealed packets rice paper can be purchased from Oriental food stores. Oriental rice paper should not be confused with the fine, wafer-like rice paper used for confectionery.

Palm sugar:
This is a rich, aromatic sugar extracted from the sap of various palms. The palm sugar used in Thailand is lighter and more refined than that used in other parts of Asia. Palm sugar is available from Oriental food shops.

RICE

Rice is the central dish of any Thai meal and the other dishes are considered to be side dishes.

Jasmine rice: For an authentic Thai meal serve steamed jasmine rice – cooked without salt. Jasmine rice is also called Thai fragrant rice and as its name suggests is delicately scented.

White glutinous rice:
This rice can either be long or short grained and is sometimes called sweet or sticky rice. For savoury dishes, Thai cooks would use the long grain variety. Glutinous rice is very high in starch content, the cooked grains cling together in a mass and are soft and sticky. Short grain white glutinous rice is mainly used for desserts.

Snake (yard-long) beans:
As their name suggests these are very long thin green beans. They are known by a variety of names including asparagus bean, pea bean, cow pea and China pea and it is the dried seeds of this bean which become black-eyed peas. If unavailable ordinary green beans can be used.

Tamarind:
This is the large pod of the tamarind or Indian date tree. After picking, it is seeded and peeled then pressed into a dark brown pulp. To use, soak the pulp in water, then strain and use as directed in the recipe. The usual dilution is three parts water to one part tamarind. There is also a tamarind concentrate available, if using this it should be diluted with double the amount of water that you would use when diluting the pulp. Tamarind is available from Indian food shops. If unavailable, use a mixture of lime or lemon juice and treacle as a substitute.

INDEX